W9-BEL-666

THE GREENHOUSE EFFECT

© Aladdin Books Ltd 1990

All rights reserved

First published in
the United States in 1990 by
Gloucester Press
387 Park Avenue South
New York NY 10016

ISBN 0-531-17217-1

Library of Congress Catalog
Card Number: 89-81605

Printed in Belgium

The publishers would like to
acknowledge that the
photographs reproduced within
this book have been posed by
models or have been obtained
from photographic agencies.

Design	David West Children's Book Design
Editor	Nicholas de Vere
Researcher	Cecilia Weston-Baker
Illustrator	Aziz Khan

The author, Dr Tony Hare, is a
writer, ecologist and TV
presenter. He works with several
environmental organizations
including the London Wildlife
Trust, the British Association of
Nature Conservationists and
Plantlife, of which he is Chairman
of the Board.

The consultants: Stewart Boyle is
Energy and Environment
Program Director at the
Association for Conservation of
Energy.

Jacky Karas is a senior Research
Associate at the Climatic Research
Unit at the University of East
Anglia.

SAVE OUR EARTH

THE GREENHOUSE EFFECT

TONY HARE

GLOUCESTER PRESS

New York · London · Toronto · Sydney

CONTENTS

INTRODUCTION

The Earth's temperature is just right for life; not too hot, like Venus, nor too cold, like Mars. In the temperatures we enjoy on our planet life can exist in abundance.

The Earth is warmed by the heat of the Sun, with the atmosphere helping by holding in some of the heat so that it does not escape into space.

This delicate balance may now be upset as a result of the pollution of the atmosphere by gases that may trap more heat close to the Earth's surface. Global temperatures have increased over the last century and this could cause widespread climate changes. A rise in sea level and other environmental changes pose a real threat to the lives of people and wildlife.

The "greenhouse effect" is the term that is used to explain how the Earth keeps warm, and how this global warming may take place. It is vital to all of us that we fully understand the complex relationship between the atmosphere and the Earth.

◄ Power stations like this one burn fossil fuel, which is itself in limited supply. The burning of fossil fuels creates pollution by putting large amounts of carbon dioxide into the atmosphere, helping to increase the greenhouse effect.

OUR EARTH

The Earth is like an island of life in empty space. Scientists do not believe that there is life anywhere else in our solar system, but here on our planet conditions are just right for life. There is plenty of water and air, and the Sun bathes us in life-giving light and warmth.

Surrounding the Earth is the atmosphere. It is a thin covering of gases, mainly nitrogen and oxygen, which extends to about 440 miles above the Earth's surface. The atmosphere keeps the Earth's surface warm and generates our weather. It also contains chemicals, such as nitrogen, carbon and sulfur, which are being constantly transferred and used by life on Earth.

Temperatures found on the Earth are suitable for animals and plants to survive and thrive. Temperatures vary across the Earth, from the cold, icy wastes of the polar regions to the heat of the deserts and tropical rain forests. But living things have adapted to all kinds of conditions, and there is life almost everywhere on the Earth.

▼ Volcanoes, like Mount St. Helens, below, produce carbon dioxide and other gases when they erupt. Carbon dioxide is important for life on Earth. Animals breathe it out, and plants take it up and use it to produce the substances they need to live and grow. It also plays a vital role in the atmosphere, helping to keep the planet warm.

Viewed from space, it is possible to see the weather patterns on the Earth. The Earth's rotation and differences in temperature cause air movements across the Earth's surface, and these in turn cause wind, cloud and rain to form. Clouds carry the rain that fills our rivers and lakes. The temperatures on Earth keep water liquid — if the Earth were too cold our water would all turn to ice, and if it were too hot the water would turn to water vapor.

THE GREENHOUSE EFFECT

The Earth is heated by the Sun's energy. When this energy reaches the Earth's atmosphere, some of it is reflected back to space, a little is absorbed, and the rest reaches the Earth, warming up its surface.

However, when heat energy comes back *from* the Earth something different happens. Instead of just passing through the atmosphere and off into space, a lot of this energy is absorbed by the gases in the atmosphere. This helps to keep the planet warm.

So the Earth's atmosphere allows sunlight through to heat the Earth, but traps the warmth that radiates back toward space. This is similar to the way a greenhouse works – except a greenhouse uses glass instead of gas – and that is why it is called the greenhouse effect.

The greenhouse gases in the atmosphere have the effect of maintaining the right average temperature on Earth, even though temperatures may vary from one part to another. Should too many of these gases be present in the atmosphere, then too much warmth could be trapped, causing the Earth's temperature to increase.

▼ **Animals need warmth to live. The polar bear (below left), like us and all other mammals, uses energy from food to keep its body warm inside. But it still needs a thick coat to keep warm enough in the Arctic. Reptiles, like the monitor lizard (below), cannot keep their bodies warm efficiently themselves, and depend on the direct heat of the Sun to warm up.**

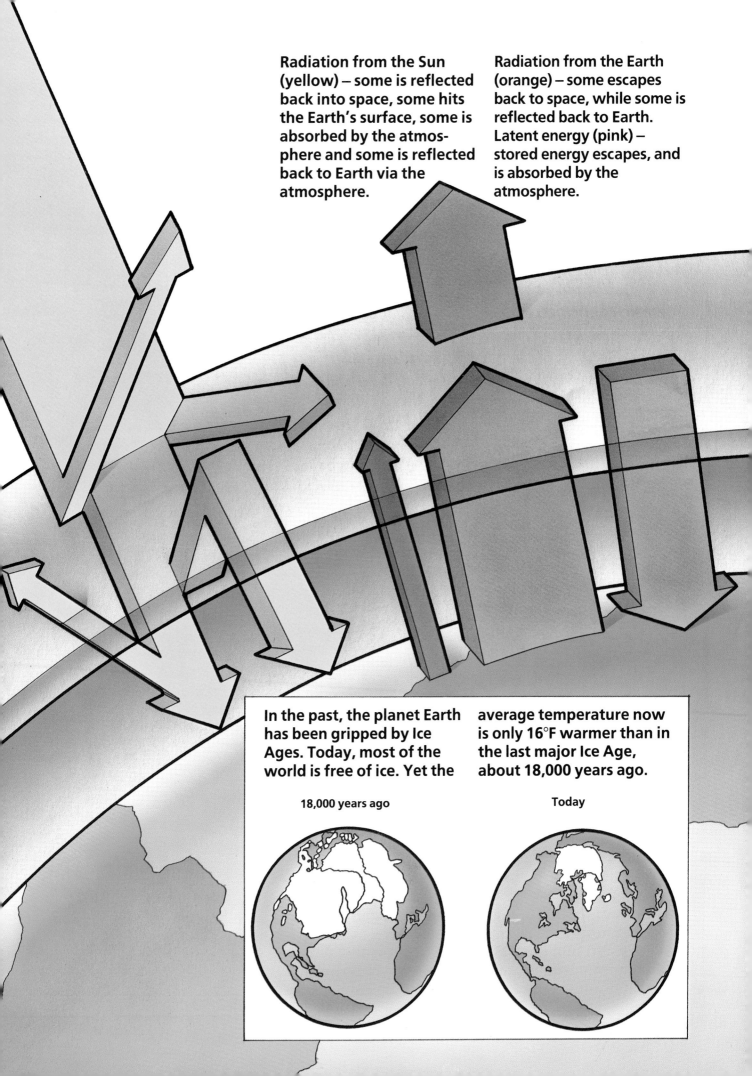

Radiation from the Sun (yellow) – some is reflected back into space, some hits the Earth's surface, some is absorbed by the atmosphere and some is reflected back to Earth via the atmosphere.

Radiation from the Earth (orange) – some escapes back to space, while some is reflected back to Earth. **Latent energy (pink)** – stored energy escapes, and is absorbed by the atmosphere.

In the past, the planet Earth has been gripped by Ice Ages. Today, most of the world is free of ice. Yet the average temperature now is only 16°F warmer than in the last major Ice Age, about 18,000 years ago.

18,000 years ago

Today

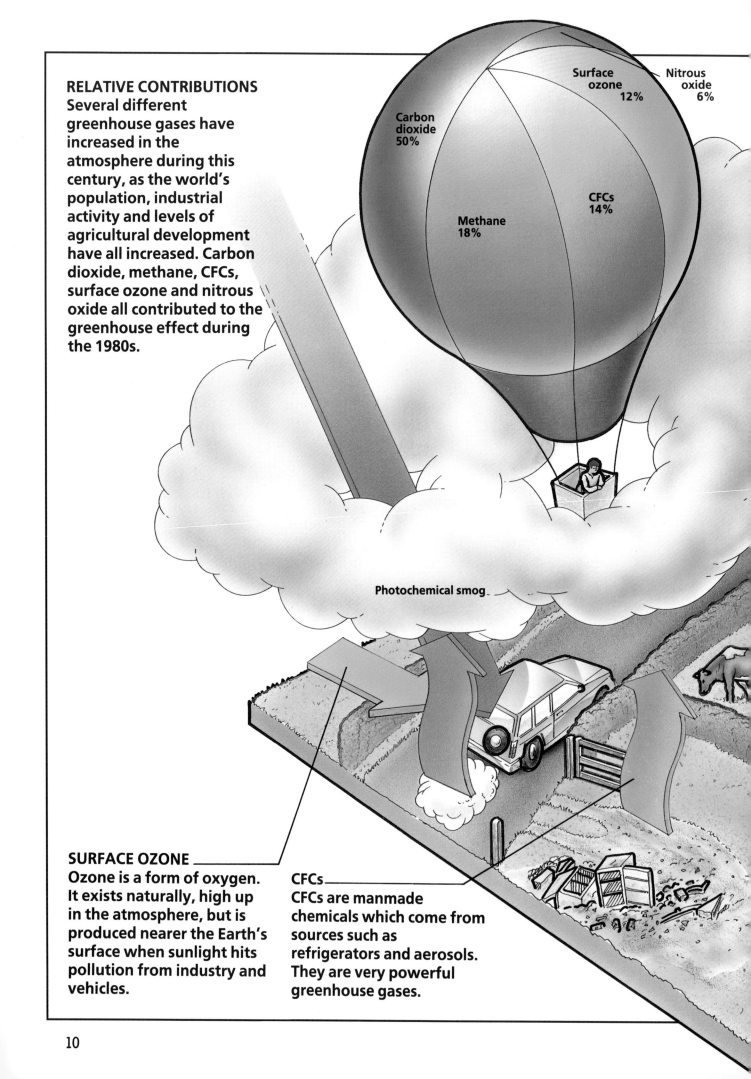

RELATIVE CONTRIBUTIONS
Several different greenhouse gases have increased in the atmosphere during this century, as the world's population, industrial activity and levels of agricultural development have all increased. Carbon dioxide, methane, CFCs, surface ozone and nitrous oxide all contributed to the greenhouse effect during the 1980s.

Carbon dioxide
50%

Surface ozone
12%

Nitrous oxide
6%

CFCs
14%

Methane
18%

Photochemical smog

SURFACE OZONE
Ozone is a form of oxygen. It exists naturally, high up in the atmosphere, but is produced nearer the Earth's surface when sunlight hits pollution from industry and vehicles.

CFCs
CFCs are manmade chemicals which come from sources such as refrigerators and aerosols. They are very powerful greenhouse gases.

STOKING THE FURNACE

How does the atmosphere trap the energy being radiated out from the planet Earth? The atmosphere contains a number of gases – many of them in very tiny amounts – which trap the heat radiated by the Earth. Carbon dioxide, methane, nitrous oxide, water vapor and ozone all occur naturally in the atmosphere and all are important greenhouse gases.

There are also manmade substances in the atmosphere which add to the greenhouse effect, like CFCs – chemicals which are also responsible for damage to the Earth's life-protecting ozone layer.

Without two naturally-occurring greenhouse gases – carbon dioxide and water vapor – the Earth would be about 90°F cooler than it is today, but by polluting the atmosphere we are increasing the quantities of the greenhouse gases and risk making the Earth overheat.

CARBON DIOXIDE
Carbon dioxide is the main greenhouse gas. It occurs naturally in the atmosphere, but human activities, especially burning fuels and deforestation, are increasing its quantities.

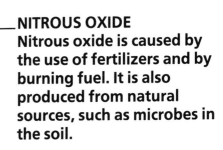

NITROUS OXIDE
Nitrous oxide is caused by the use of fertilizers and by burning fuel. It is also produced from natural sources, such as microbes in the soil.

METHANE
Methane is a smelly gas from swampy places, such as rice paddies and waste dumps, and is also produced by cattle.

CO$_2$ – THE MAIN CULPRIT

Coal, oil and natural gas are all fossil fuels. We burn them – in the home, in factories, in cars and in power stations – to produce heat and energy. They are called fossil fuels because they have been formed over the course of millions of years from the remains of plants and animals buried in the ground.

However, fossil fuels contain large amounts of carbon, and when they are burned they release energy that has been locked away for millions of years. Every bit we burn releases carbon dioxide – CO$_2$ – into the atmosphere and adds to the greenhouse effect.

Fossil fuels are not the only things that are being burned and producing carbon dioxide. The world's rain forests are being burned to clear land for agriculture. Rain forest destruction is a tragedy for the Earth. It releases huge quantities of CO$_2$ into the atmosphere and it removes trees that would normally take up CO$_2$ – so it makes a double contribution to the greenhouse effect. The forests have given us many vital drugs and are the home to vanishing tribes and a multitude of wildlife.

▼ **The picture below shows a typical scene from the Amazon, where huge acres of irreplaceable tropical rain forest are being burned to make way for agriculture. The inset map shows where the tropical rain forests are found throughout the world.**

Areas of tropical rain forest

CARBON EMISSIONS WORLDWIDE FROM FOSSIL FUELS

1,013.6

247.5

355.2

791.6

365.7

146.0

314.7

150.4

1,224.0

105.6

152.6

229.7

50.2

Canada
USA
Brazil
Latin America
Western Europe
Eastern Europe
USSR
Middle East
Africa
India
China
Japan
Oceana

Carbon emissions in millions of metric tons

The industrial nations of Europe and North America produce far more CO$_2$ than the developing nations.

OTHER CULPRITS

Carbon dioxide is the main greenhouse gas, but there are a number of others. Over 30 have so far been identified, and there are likely to be others that we are not yet aware of.

The quantities of many of the greenhouse gases in the atmosphere are quite small, but unfortunately, their power as heat-trappers is frightening. Methane is estimated to be about 30 times as effective as carbon dioxide, nitrous oxide 150 times, surface ozone 2,000 times, and CFCs an incredible 10-23,000 times.

What makes this worse is that some of the greenhouse gases have very long lives in the atmosphere – though surface ozone lasts only a few weeks, nitrous oxide can last up to 170 years. Most CFCs are expected to last for about a century, but some may last as long as 20,000 years. Statistics like these prove that we are going to have to live with – and deal with – global warming for a long time to come.

Methane comes from grazing animals, such as cows, as a waste product, and is increasing as we keep more and more cattle; the number of cattle in the world doubled between 1960 and 1980. Methane is also known as marsh gas, and is the gas that bubbles up and smells bad in wet, swampy places, such as rice paddies. It is released from waste dumps when buried garbage rots, and it also leaks from coal mines and natural gas pipes. The amount of methane in the atmosphere now is more than double what it was before the industrial age began.

× **30**

Nitrous oxide is naturally present in the atmosphere, and is produced and consumed by living things in soil and water. It is produced when forests are burned, by vehicle exhausts, and from artificial fertilizers which farmers use all over the world. The amount of nitrous oxide in the atmosphere is estimated to have risen by about 80% since the start of the century.

$\times$ **150**

CFCs are used in aerosols, in refrigerators, in the plastic foam industry and in the air-conditioners that are used in hot climates. CFCs escape into the atmosphere from these sources. Unfortunately, some of the chemicals, called hydrocarbons, which are used in "ozone-friendly" aerosols that do not damage the ozone layer, are also greenhouse gases.

$\times$ **10,000+**

Surface ozone Ozone high in the atmosphere forms the ozone layer, which protects the Earth from dangerous ultraviolet radiation from the Sun. But ozone at lower levels is a pollutant, helping to form photochemical smog and adding to the greenhouse effect. Unfortunately, ozone at the lower levels of the atmosphere gets stuck there and cannot drift up toward the ozone layer.

$\times$ **2,000**

GLOBAL WARMING

The weather seems to change every day, and a difference of a few degrees between one day and the next seems very little. However, in terms of the Earth's average temperature, a few degrees is a very big difference.

Scientists think that a doubling of greenhouse gases could lead to a global warming of between 6°F to 18°F. Since the difference between the last great Ice Age and the present day is only 16°F it is not hard to imagine that a global increase now of about the same amount might have catastrophic results. All over the world conditions would change. Temperatures in the United Kingdom could become like those the Mediterranean countries at present, meaning a complete change in the crops grown and a greater likelihood of droughts.

The greenhouse effect might, in the short term, help parts of the world – for example, farming in Siberia. But here the melting of the permafrost might also release stored amounts of methane gas.

▼ The diagram below left shows how the average temperature has increased since the 1800s. On the right, the timescale is much greater, and shows scientist's predictions of global warming by the end of the next century.

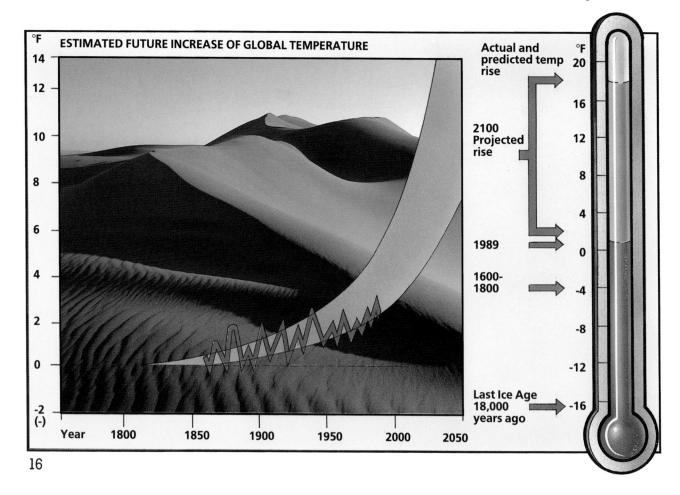

ESTIMATED FUTURE INCREASE OF GLOBAL TEMPERATURE

Actual and predicted temp rise

2100 Projected rise

1989

1600-1800

Last Ice Age 18,000 years ago

The drought in the United States (top right) and the floods in Bangladesh are examples of extreme climatic conditions today. Global warming won't simply make the world a slightly warmer, sunnier place to live; the effects are much more complicated. The warming, which is expected to be greatest toward the poles, will severely disrupt the world's weather systems. There is evidence of a warm period 6-9,000 years ago, and the map below shows projected climate changes of a new global warming.

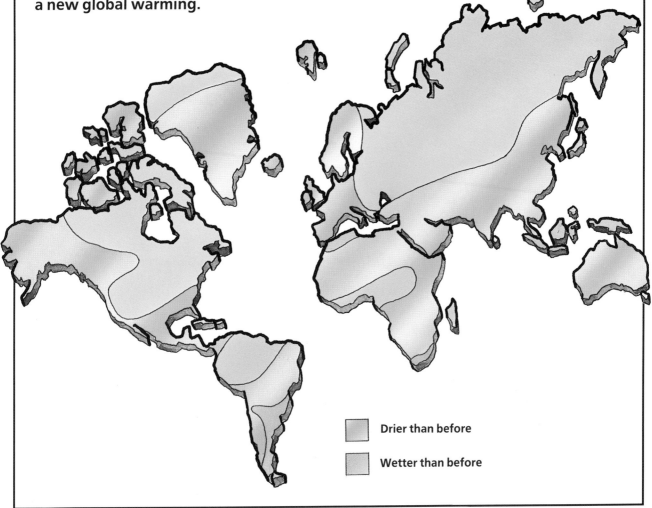

Drier than before

Wetter than before

RISING SEA LEVELS

If the world warms up, glaciers on mountains, and the ice caps of the North Pole and Antarctica, could start melting. Nobody knows exactly how much sea levels might rise. But if nothing is done to stop global warming, then they might increase by 8 to 16 inches by early in the next century, and could then continue to rise.

Even a small sea level rise could have catastrophic results for low-lying countries. Much of the land in the Netherlands has been reclaimed from the sea and is very low-lying. A rise in sea level could put great stretches of the country under water or force the building of expensive new sea walls. The Maldives, in the Indian Ocean, are very low-lying too, and would almost completely disappear under the waves if the sea level rose by about three feet. The effects of a 12-24 feet rise in sea level would be even more disastrous.

▼ **In London, the Thames Barrier has been designed to prevent major floods, but poorer countries cannot afford such sophisticated defenses. In the long term, if nothing is done, sea levels may rise enough to swamp large areas of land everywhere, even in countries like the United States, which have plenty of resources to fight the elements.**

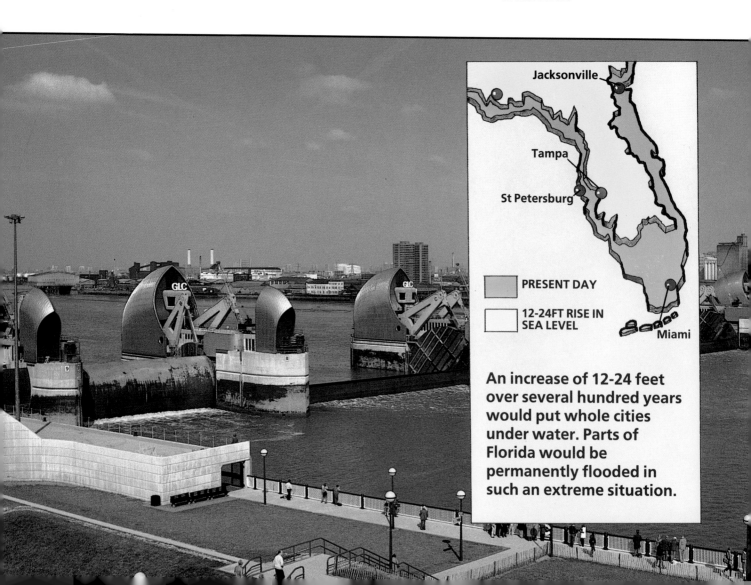

Jacksonville

Tampa

St Petersburg

Miami

PRESENT DAY

12-24FT RISE IN SEA LEVEL

An increase of 12-24 feet over several hundred years would put whole cities under water. Parts of Florida would be permanently flooded in such an extreme situation.

▼ Bangladesh has suffered many floods. Rising sea levels would make the situation even more desperate.

▲ The gradual melting of the ice caps would pour water into the seas, making them considerably deeper.

THE EVIDENCE

How do we know the amounts of greenhouse gases in the atmosphere are rising and that the world's temperature is rising?

Bubbles of air trapped long ago in the ice sheets of Greenland and Antarctica can be compared with modern-day air. Results show that the concentrations of greenhouse gases have been steadily rising in recent years. Weather observations taken over many years show that average global temperatures have risen by about two degrees Fahrenheit in the last 100 years.

Some people believe that recent natural disasters – drought in the United States, floods in Bangladesh, and hurricanes in the Caribbean – are the result of the climatic disruption already being caused by global warming. However, such events could have occurred naturally. The most compelling evidence so far that the climate may be changing is that during the 1980s the world had six of the hottest years ever recorded. The next few years may provide further evidence.

▶ Recent years have seen a worldwide spate of terrible hurricanes. The Great Storm of 1987 was the worst storm recorded in the United Kingdom. Hurricane Gilbert (right), which left almost a quarter of Jamaica's people homeless in 1988, was the most severe hurricane on record.

◀ On the Mauna Loa volcano, in Hawaii, where the air is exceptionally clear, an atmospheric monitoring station was established in the 1950s. The recordings of carbon dioxide levels taken at Mauna Loa since its establishment, show the levels of this greenhouse gas in the atmosphere has been creeping gradually higher, year by year.

Natural disasters come in all shapes and forms, and are often associated with climatic factors like rainfall – or lack of it – and temperature. Records show that the number of natural disasters and freak weather conditions has increased over the last three decades.

1960s

1970s

1980s

FLOODS

STORMS

DROUGHT

FREAK TEMP

AVERAGE RECORDED NATURAL DISASTERS WORLDWIDE

WHAT CAN BE DONE?

If we are to avoid the potential problems of global warming, the first thing we must do is to cut back the amount of greenhouse gases getting into, and poisoning, the atmosphere.

To reduce carbon dioxide levels, we must start by burning less fossil fuels. We can do this by using alternative sources of energy, like wind, wave and solar power. Conserving and being more efficient with energy are also really effective ways to cut down the amount of carbon dioxide getting into the atmosphere. If we use less energy in the home and in industry, less fossil fuels will have to be burned in power stations and boilers.

Another way we can reduce the level of carbon dioxide is to stop cutting down and burning forests. We can also plant trees – they absorb carbon dioxide and prevent it from getting into the atmosphere.

Many people all over the world oppose the senseless destruction of the world's rain forests, and make their feelings known by marching and demonstrating.

▼ Sting and his cameraman are seen here with local Brazilian tribesmen, whose livelihoods are being threatened by the destruction of the tropical rain forests.

△ We have to cut out the use of CFCs altogether. Aerosols are a major source of CFCs, and there are already many environment-friendly sprays. We must find ways of replacing, recycling or getting rid of CFCs in other areas too. With methane, as the picture left shows, a plant can extract reusable gas from animal waste.

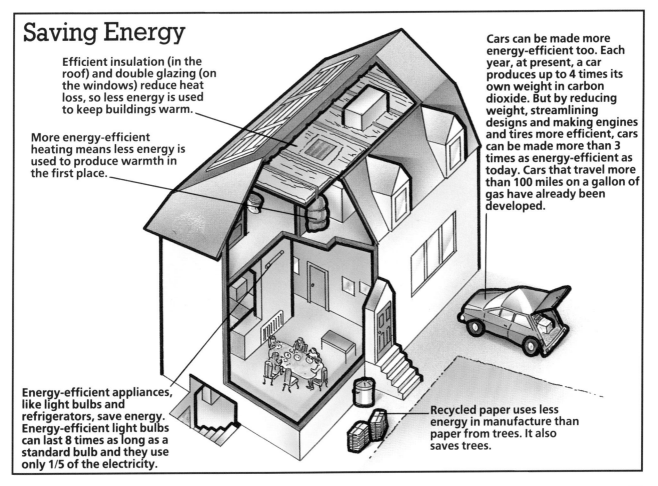

Saving Energy

Efficient insulation (in the roof) and double glazing (on the windows) reduce heat loss, so less energy is used to keep buildings warm.

More energy-efficient heating means less energy is used to produce warmth in the first place.

Energy-efficient appliances, like light bulbs and refrigerators, save energy. Energy-efficient light bulbs can last 8 times as long as a standard bulb and they use only 1/5 of the electricity.

Cars can be made more energy-efficient too. Each year, at present, a car produces up to 4 times its own weight in carbon dioxide. But by reducing weight, streamlining designs and making engines and tires more efficient, cars can be made more than 3 times as energy-efficient as today. Cars that travel more than 100 miles on a gallon of gas have already been developed.

Recycled paper uses less energy in manufacture than paper from trees. It also saves trees.

ENERGY ALTERNATIVES

All methods of energy production have hazards associated with them – particularly nuclear energy. It is important to minimize energy usage through conservation and efficiency, while at the same time reducing the impact on the environment of energy production.

There are other ways of generating energy which do not burn any fossil fuel. They include wind power, solar power, biomass burning, wave power and hydroelectric power. Nuclear power is another alternative, but is controversial due to the risks involved.

These ways of generating energy produce about 20 percent of the world's energy requirements at the moment, but if we were to turn to them for more energy we could eventually cut fossil-fuel burning drastically.

Wind power: **wind turbines – tall machines looking like huge windmills – can be used to harness the power of the wind. Their blades turn in the wind and drive a generator to make electricity.**

Nuclear power: **although nuclear power – power produced from the forces that actually hold matter together – seems like the perfect answer to energy needs, it has many problems – especially the disposal of nuclear waste and the potentially disastrous effects of nuclear accidents.**

Geothermal power: **in certain volcanic regions, hot springs and fountains of steam provide energy for heating and generating electricity.**

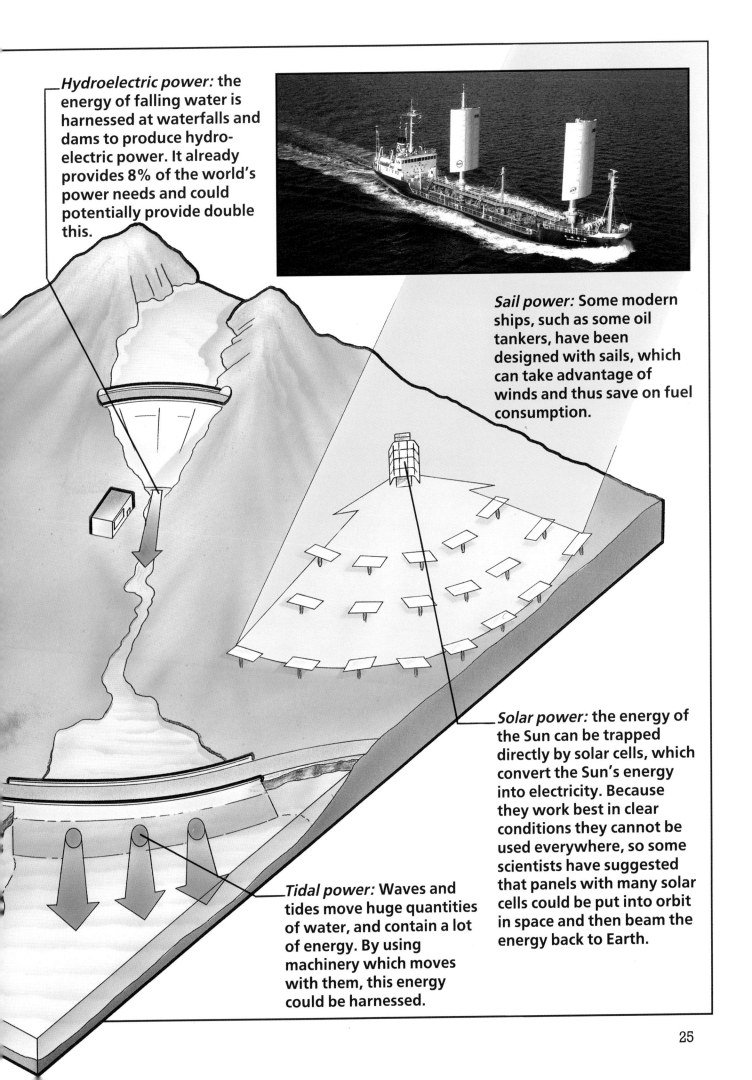

Hydroelectric power: the energy of falling water is harnessed at waterfalls and dams to produce hydro-electric power. It already provides 8% of the world's power needs and could potentially provide double this.

Sail power: Some modern ships, such as some oil tankers, have been designed with sails, which can take advantage of winds and thus save on fuel consumption.

Solar power: the energy of the Sun can be trapped directly by solar cells, which convert the Sun's energy into electricity. Because they work best in clear conditions they cannot be used everywhere, so some scientists have suggested that panels with many solar cells could be put into orbit in space and then beam the energy back to Earth.

Tidal power: Waves and tides move huge quantities of water, and contain a lot of energy. By using machinery which moves with them, this energy could be harnessed.

WHAT YOU CAN DO

There is plenty we can all do at home and in our lives to help prevent the greenhouse effect.

* Improve insulation and heating at home.
* Use energy-efficient appliances.
* Use energy-efficient light bulbs in your room.
* Switch off lights and heating when they are not needed.
* Use public transportation as much as possible.
* Don't use aerosols.
* Use recycled paper.

Useful addresses:

Global ReLeaf
P.O. Box 2000
Washington, D.C. 20013

The Greenhouse Crisis Foundation
1130 17 St, Nw
Washington, D.C. 20036

Environmental Defense Fund
257 Park Avenue South, Suite 16
New York, NY 10016

Sierra Club
730 Folk Street
San Francisco, CA 94109

The Union of Concerned Scientists
26 Church Street
Cambridge, MA 02238

National Science Foundation
1800 G Street, N.W.
Washington, DC 20550

Designing a poster:

One of the most important things that can be done is to make more people aware of the greenhouse effect. One way you can do this is to make a poster to hang up on a school notice board or in your bedroom.

1) Think up a striking or clever heading for the poster which will grab the attention of the viewers.

2) Design an illustration or symbol like the one shown here or cut pictures out of magazines and make a collage that conveys the main message.

3) Read through this book and try to summarize in about 30 – 40 words what is happening with the greenhouse effect and why it is important.

4) Again by reading through the book, make some suggestions as to what can be done to prevent the greenhouse effect.

5) Include some other information if there is room – such as useful addresses to contact for more information, and symbols that are printed on ozone-friendly items.

THE GREENHOUSE EFFECT

1

2

3

THE ACCUMULATION OF HARMFUL GASES, WHICH ARE CAPABLE OF DESTROYING THE OZONE LAYER, CAN RESULT IN GLOBAL WARMING

IF THIS CONTINUES OUR EARTH WILL BE DAMAGED BEYOND ALL REPAIR!

WHAT CAN YOU DO?

4

- THE MOST DAMAGING GAS IS CARBON DIOXIDE WHICH IS PRODUCED BY BURNING FOSSIL FUELS AND TREES. SWITCHING OFF LIGHTS AND OTHER APPLIANCES WHEN THEY ARE NOT NEEDED WOULD

5

SAVE ENERGY AND REDUCE THE AMOUNT OF FUEL BEING BURNT IN POWER STATIONS.
- TRY TO USE RECYCLED PAPER
- DON'T USE AEROSOLS WHICH CONTAIN CFCs
- CONTACT YOUR LOCAL GREENPEACE OR FRIENDS OF THE EARTH BRANCHES

USEFUL ADDRESSES

FACT FILES

Radiation and cloud cover – Radiation from the Sun travels by short wavelengths in the visible part of the spectrum, and is largely not absorbed by the atmosphere. The Earth radiates back heat in longer wavelengths, which bounce off the atmosphere. Much of this heat is absorbed by the atmosphere and reflects back to Earth.

Global warming may cause an increase in cloud cover, which may play a part in both increasing the greenhouse effect (by trapping heat and reflecting it back to Earth), and in decreasing it (by reflecting solar energy back out to space).

Solar radiation (shortwave)

Atmosphere

Radiation from the Earth (longwave)

Earth

Life in the atmosphere – The various greenhouse gases can stay in the atmosphere for a long time before they are eventually broken down into other substances or leave the atmosphere. Many CFCs may remain there for perhaps as long as a century, and some CFCs may last as

long as 20,000 years.

All this means that we have to stop putting greenhouse gases into the atmosphere *NOW* – there are already enough greenhouse gases up there which are on their way to having a very serious effect over the next few decades.

Gases life

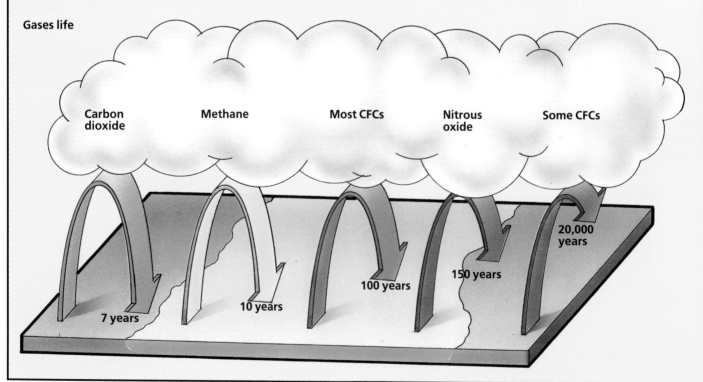

Carbon dioxide

Methane

Most CFCs

Nitrous oxide

Some CFCs

20,000 years

150 years

100 years

10 years

7 years

Energy-efficient public transportation – Look around and see how many cars have just one person riding in them. If there were more buses and trains for us to use, and if we used them instead of taking the car out for everything, we'd really be helping to prevent the greenhouse effect.

A bus produces more carbon dioxide pollution than a car, but if you think of there being, say, 20 passengers on a bus and often only 1 in a car, the car driver is responsible for up to 4 times as much pollution as each bus passenger.

The carbon cycle – Carbon dioxide plays a vital role in life on Earth. It is one form of carbon, which is an important part of many of the substances that animals and plants use for food and energy.

Plants use carbon dioxide from the atmosphere to obtain carbon. Animals obtain their carbon by eating plants and other animals. Carbon is released again to return to the atmosphere as carbon dioxide when plants and animals die and

rot, when plants are burned and when animals breathe.

Some carbon dioxide is absorbed by the oceans, which altogether hold a huge quantity of it. Not counting the carbon held in the sediments at the bottoms of the oceans, the oceans still hold about 50 times as much carbon as the atmosphere. It may be that the oceans could help slow down global warming by absorbing the extra CO_2 we are producing.

Carbon dioxide producers – About 80% of carbon dioxide pollution comes from the burning of fossil fuels. The United Kingdom produces 3% of the world's carbon dioxide from fossil fuels – though it has only 1% of the world's population. North America produces 25%, western Europe as a whole 15%, eastern Europe 23%, China 11% and other developing countries 16%.

In the United States, the main sources of carbon dioxide pollution are electricity generation, industry, and transportation.

Another greenhouse in space – Venus has an atmosphere very rich in carbon dioxide. This keeps it very warm indeed – too hot for life to exist.

Proof that energy can be saved – In Denmark, the amount of energy needed to heat buildings has been reduced by 35% over the last 15 years. The Danes use combined heat and power stations (known as cogeneration stations) which are more than twice as efficient as the power stations used in the UK. In the United States, the law is being used against global warming; the 1987 Appliances Efficiency Act is calculated to save 55 million tons of CO_2 per year by the year 2000.

The effect isn't new – We have been putting carbon dioxide into the atmosphere for centuries, but the amounts have increased since the birth of the Industrial Age. In fact, scientists say that the world has already warmed by about two degrees Fahrenheit in the last century and is continuing to warm up.

GLOSSARY

Alternative energy sources – Energy sources which produce energy without burning fossil fuels. They include solar energy, wind energy and hydroelectric energy.

CFCs – Chlorofluorocarbons; chemicals which are used for a variety of applications, including aerosols, refrigerators and the manufacture of some types of foam packaging.

Energy – Energy is the ability to do work. It comes in many different forms. We have to generate it in order to use many of the objects which we consider to be vital in the modern world – from light bulbs to motor cars. For a very long time we have produced energy by burning wood, coal, oil and gas. But in recent years, people have looked at the possiblity of using alternative energy sources.

Energy-efficient products – Products which use the minimum amount of energy to do their jobs, therefore saving energy and money. By saving energy they can also help to prevent an increase in the greenhouse effect, because they reduce the amount of energy which has to be generated in the first place, and therefore potentially cut down the amount of fossil fuel burned at power stations.

Fossil fuels – Coal, oil and natural gas: these substances have been buried or trapped beneath the ground for millions of years; they originate from the remains of living creatures, both plant and animal. When they are burned they release energy.

Global warming – Atmospheric pollution has increased the greenhouse effect by putting more gases that trap heat into the atmosphere. This is causing the Earth's temperature to rise; an effect known as global warming.

Greenhouse effect – The warming effect of the Earth's atmosphere. Some gases in the atmosphere allow energy from the Sun to pass through to warm the Earth's surface, and then trap the heat coming back. This keeps the atmosphere – and the planet – warm. It is known as the greenhouse effect and helps to make life on Earth possible.

Greenhouse gases – The gases which cause the greenhouse effect. Many of them occur naturally in the atmosphere – for example carbon dioxide, ozone and methane – but others, such as CFCs, are only there because of human activities.

INDEX

Photographic Credits:
Cover: Zefa; pages 4/5 and 6: Science Photo Library; page 7: NASA; pages 8 left, 15 bottom, 21 and 22: Frank Spooner Agency; pages 8 right, 13, 17 top: Rex Features; pages 12, 14, 16, 25 and 30 top: Bruce Coleman Ltd; pages 15 top and 19 bottom: Topham Picture Library; pages 18 and 23 right: Robert Harding Library; page 19 top: Eye Ubiquitous; pages 19 middle and 23 left: Roger Vlitos; page 29: Hutchison Library; page 30 bottom: Mary Evans Picture Library.